WHY WE GO TO THE DENTIST

by Rosalyn Clark

BUMBA BOOKS™

LERNER PUBLICATIONS ◆ MINNEAPOLIS

Note to Educators:

Throughout this book, you'll find critical thinking questions. These can be used to engage young readers in thinking critically about the topic and in using the text and photos to do so.

Lerner Publications Company
A division of Lerner Publishing Group, Inc.
241 First Avenue North
Minneapolis, MN 55401 USA

For reading levels and more information, look up this title at www.lernerbooks.com.

Library of Congress Cataloging-in-Publication Data

Names: Clark, Rosalyn, 1990- author.
Title: Why we go to the dentist / Rosalyn Clark.
Description: Minneapolis : Lerner Publications, [2018] | Series: Bumba books.
   Health matters | Audience: Ages 4-7. | Audience: K to grade 3. | Includes
   bibliographical references and index.
Identifiers: LCCN 2017019799 (print) | LCCN 2017026529 (ebook) | ISBN
   9781512482980 (eb pdf) | ISBN 9781512482928 (lb : alk. paper) | ISBN
   9781541511088 (pb : alk. paper)
Subjects: LCSH: Dentistry--Juvenile literature. | Dentists--Juvenile
   literature.
Classification: LCC RK63 (ebook) | LCC RK63 .C53 2018 (print) | DDC
   617.6--dc23

LC record available at https://lccn.loc.gov/2017019799

Manufactured in the United States of America
1 – CG – 12/31/17

Expand learning beyond the printed book. Download free, complementary educational resources for this book from our website, www.lerneresource.com.

Table of Contents

Going to the Dentist 4

Things We
See at the Dentist 22

Picture Glossary 23

Read More 24

Index 24

Going to the Dentist

Today we are going to the

dentist's office.

It is time for a checkup.

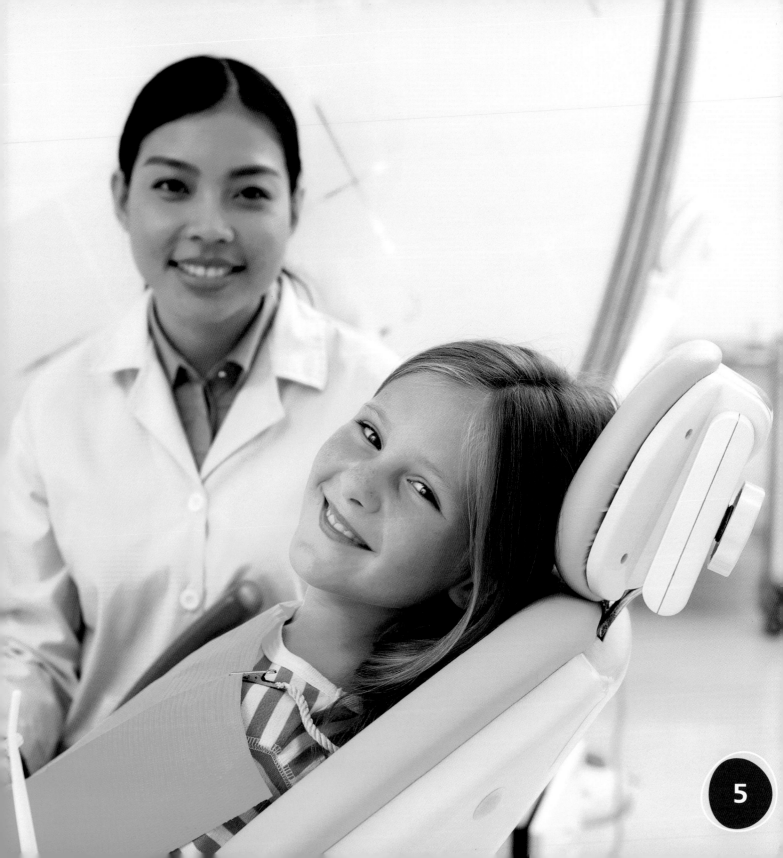

Dentists know all about what is inside your mouth.

They help keep your mouth healthy.

Dentists check your teeth.

Your teeth are important.

They help you chew food.

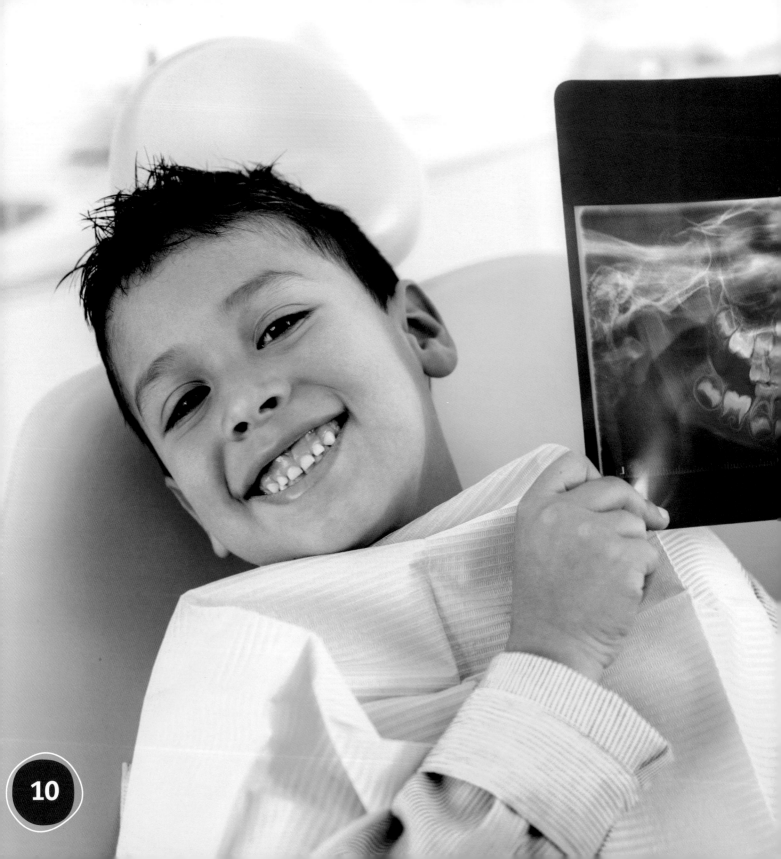

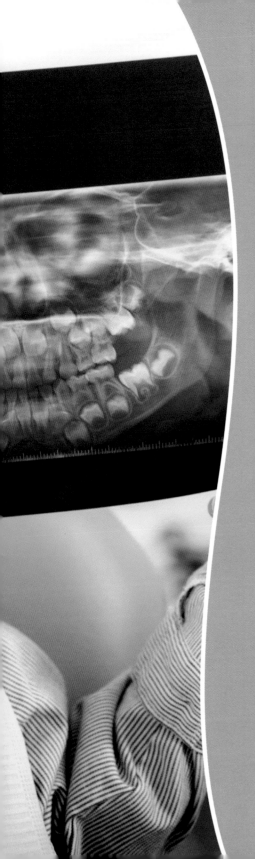

Dentists take X-rays

of your teeth.

They look for cavities.

How do you think X-rays help dentists check your mouth?

Dentists also check your gums.

Gums protect your teeth.

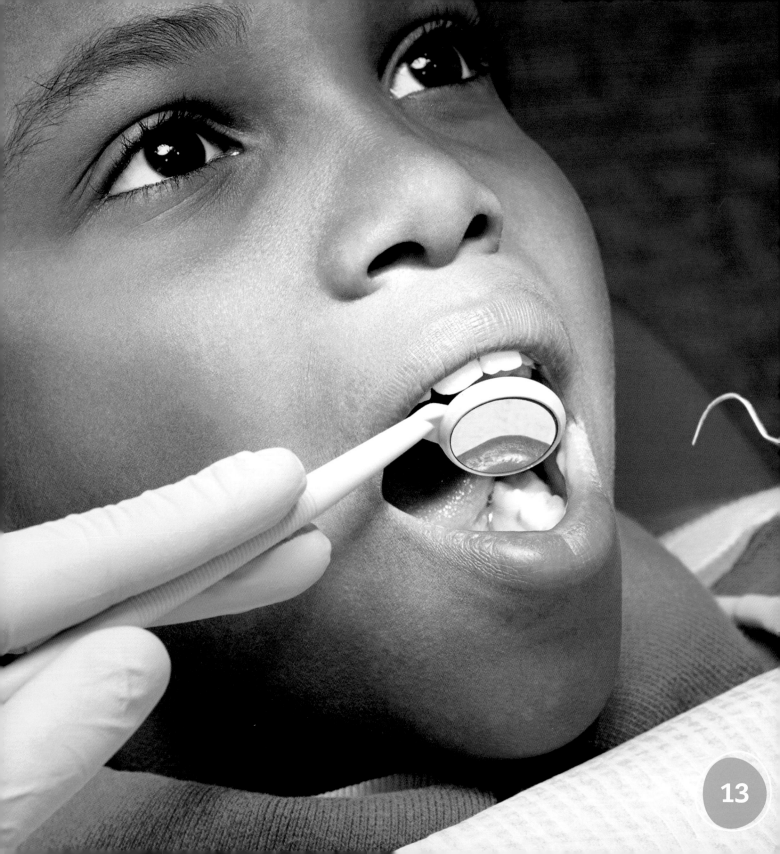

Dentists clean your teeth.

They show you how to floss.

Why do you think you need to floss your teeth?

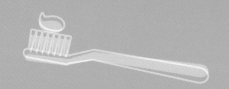

Dentists show you how to brush your teeth.

Bacteria can grow on teeth.

Brushing gets rid of bacteria.

Do you know how often you should brush your teeth?

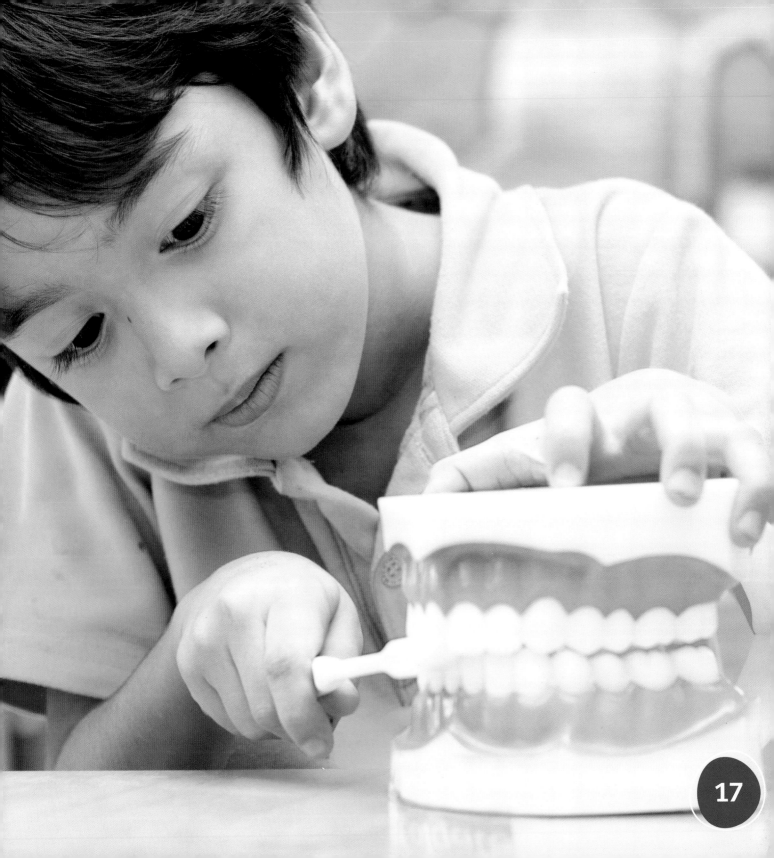

We are all done at the dentist!

Dentists give you a toothbrush and

some floss at the end of your visit.

Dentists care about you.

They work hard to keep your teeth and gums healthy.

Things We See at the Dentist

light

X-rays

tools

chair

dentist

Picture Glossary

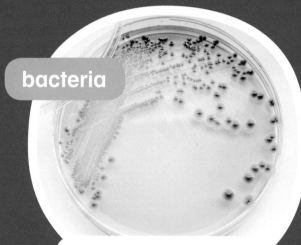

bacteria

living things that can cause disease

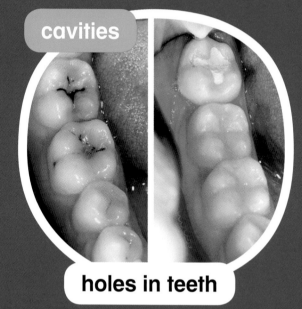

cavities

holes in teeth

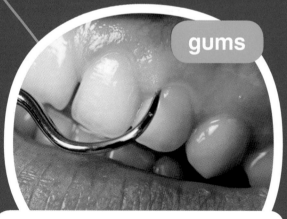

gums

the areas of skin around the roots of teeth

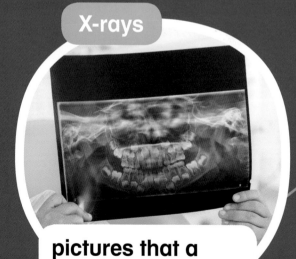

X-rays

pictures that a doctor or dentist takes of something inside your body

Read More

Hewitt, Sally. *Going to the Dentist*. Irvine, CA: QEB Publishing, 2015.

Kenan, Tessa. *Hooray for Dentists!* Minneapolis: Lerner Publications, 2018.

Lee, David. *My Visit to the Dentist*. New York: PowerKids Press, 2017.

Index

bacteria, 16

brush, 16

cavities, 11

clean, 15

floss, 15, 19

gums, 12, 20

X-rays, 11

Photo Credits

The images in this book are used with the permission of: © Dragonimages/iStock.com, p. 5; © wowsty/Shutterstock.com, p. 6; © didesign021/Shutterstock.com, p. 9; © andresr/iStock.com, pp. 10–11, 23 (bottom right); © XiXinXing/iStock.com, p. 13; © FangXiaNuo/iStock.com, pp. 14–15; © wckiw/iStock.com, pp. 16–17; © Brocreative/Shutterstock.com, p. 18; © XiXinXing/iStock.com, p. 21; © pathdoc/Shutterstock.com, p. 22 (right); © Chepe Nicoli/Shutterstock.com, p. 22 (left); © Sirirat/Shutterstock.com, p. 23 (top left); © Lighthunter/Shutterstock.com, p. 23 (top right); © Ocskay Bence/Shutterstock.com, p. 23 (bottom left).

Front Cover: © Evgeniy Kalinovskiy/Shutterstock.com.